Our **WILD**™
WORLD
SERIES

Snakes

NORTHWORD
Minnetonka, Minnessota

DEDICATION
For Dr. Randy Langerhans and the good people at Fort Worth Animal Medical Center
– D.D.

Photography © 2003: Brian Kenney: cover, pp. 4, 5, 7, 10-11, 12, 16, 19, 24, 28, 36; Joe McDonald/Tom Stack & Associates: p. 8; Michael H. Francis: pp. 18, 26-27, 43; Ed Reschke: pp. 20-21; Allen Blake Sheldon: pp. 23, 29, 33, 34, 35, 44; James E. Gerholdt: pp. 30-31, 40; Robert & Linda Mitchell: pp. 38-39, back cover.

Illustrations by Jennifer Owings Dewey
Designed by Russell S. Kuepper
Edited by Judy Gitenstein
Front cover image: Green tree python (*Chondropython viridis*)

NorthWord Books for Young Readers
11571 K-Tel Drive
Minnetonka, MN 55343
1-888-255-9989
www.tnkidsbooks.com

Library of Congress Cataloging-in-Publication Data

Dennard, Deborah.
      Snakes / Deborah Dennard ; illustrations by Jennifer Owings Dewey.
         p.   cm   – (Our wild world series)
      Includes index.
      Summary: Discusses the physical characteristics, behavior, habitat, and life cycle of snakes.
      ISBN 1-55971-856-0 (hardcover) – ISBN 1-55971-855-2 (softcover)
      1. Snakes—Juvenile literature. [1. Snakes.]. I. Dewey, Jennifer, ill. II. Title. III. Series.

QL666.O6D453 2003
597.96--dc21
                                                                                    2002043101

Printed in Malaysia

Snakes

Deborah Dennard
Illustrations by Jennifer Owings Dewey

NorthWord
Minnetonka, Minnessota

SNAKES ARE AMAZING animals. They come in a rainbow of colors. They are excellent hunters. Different snakes eat everything from ants to pigs. They live in many places in the world.

There are between 2,500 and 3,000 species (SPEE-sees), or kinds, of snakes in the world. Each species is perfectly suited for its own special habitat, or the type of place it lives. Snakes belong to a large group of animals that scientists call *Class Reptilia*. Snakes are reptiles. Reptiles are cold-blooded animals. This means that the temperature of a snake's body is the same as the air or water around it.

The bright, beautiful colors found in many snakes, such as this Honduran palm viper, give a warning to other animals to stay away.

African bush vipers come in 3 different colors: gray, orange, and yellow.

Many people think that snakes have slimy skin. They don't! All reptiles have dry, scaly skin. They have different types of scales on different parts of their bodies. The scales on the back and the sides of their bodies are usually in rows. In some species the scales may be small, smooth, and rounded. In other species the scales are sometimes rough and thick. They may even stick out from the body like armor or spikes.

Snakes often have scales on their bellies that are wide, flat, and smooth. This helps a snake drag itself along the ground. Scales on the head may be of different shapes and sizes. Some may be large and platelike. Others may be small and fine. Scientists use scale patterns along the back and sides of a snake to identify the species.

There are 4 main groups of reptiles. Snakes and lizards belong to a group called *Order Squamata* (skwa-MAH-tah). The second group of reptiles includes turtles and tortoises. The third group includes alligators and crocodiles. The fourth group is made up only of the tuatara (too-ah-TAR-ah), a reptile from New Zealand.

Snakes
FUNFACT:

The longest known snake in the United States was an indigo snake that measured just under 9 feet (2.7 meters) long.

Male indigo snakes are very territorial during mating season and have been known to use their teeth to make 6-inch (15-centimeter) long cuts on other males.

Anacondas are often found soaking in water.

Snakes do not have legs for walking. They slither (SLIH-thur) or glide instead of walk. Snakes do not have eyelids. Their eyes are covered in dry scales, just like the rest of their bodies. Snakes have long forked (FORKT) tongues. A forked tongue is split down the middle and has 2 sections.

Snakes come in many sizes and colors. Most are thin and small, less than 3 feet (0.9 meters) long. Some grow to be very long with thick, heavy bodies. The biggest snake in the world is the anaconda (an-uh-CON-duh) that may grow to be over 26 feet (7.9 meters) long.

Sidewinders loop their bodies as they move,
leaving an unusual track behind.

Snakes of all sizes have flexible spines and strong muscles. When they move, they flex their muscles and stretch their spines. This makes some snakes seem to weave their way across the ground in the shape of an "S."

Flexible spines and strong muscles also allow some snakes to climb trees. Others burrow underground or fit into tiny hiding places. Snakes known as sidewinders loop one part of their bodies in the air as they move. They look like they are winding sideways across the desert sands. When other snakes move, they seem to stretch themselves out, then pull themselves together, just like the folds in an accordion.

The green mamba is a highly venomous snake related to the cobra.
Its long, slender body is perfect for slithering through the treetops.

This Gaboon viper (right) has shed its skin (left).
Even the eye scales are visible in the shell of the shed skin.

All snakes shed their skin, and they do this throughout their entire lives. As they grow their old skin becomes too small. A new, larger skin grows underneath. When the old skin is ready to be shed, a snake may rub back and forth against a rock to loosen the old skin. It may soak in water to loosen the old skin. Then the snake simply slithers out of it. Scientists can look at a skin that has been shed and identify what species of snake it is from.

Some snakes swallow eggs whole and do not crush them
until the egg is in their stomachs.

Snakes are predators (PRED-uh-torz). Predators hunt and kill other animals for food. Even very small snakes hunt prey (PRAY), or animals for food. Very small snakes eat animals as tiny as ants, crickets, or worms. Medium-sized snakes eat rats, mice, or rabbits. Very large snakes eat animals as large as pigs or deer.

Snakes must be very good hunters in order to survive. Different snakes have different ways of hunting. Some snakes open their mouths very wide and even unhinge (un-HINJ), or separate, their jaws so they can eat things that are larger than their heads. Some snakes strike very quickly at their prey, grabbing it with their mouths and swallowing.

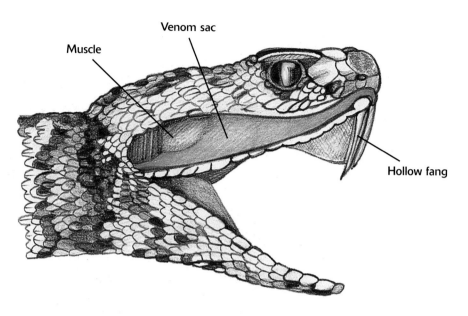

Muscle

Venom sac

Hollow fang

Venom is made and stored in large venom sacs and injected into prey
through hollow teeth called fangs. These parts are highlighted in color above.

Boas, anacondas, and pythons are constrictors. Constrictors are snakes that grab their prey with their mouths and loop their bodies around the prey. Then they squeeze until the prey cannot breathe. Once the prey is dead, constrictors stop squeezing and swallow their meal whole.

Snakes do not use their teeth for chewing. They use their teeth for jabbing, grabbing, and swallowing.

Some snakes are venomous (VEN-im-us). Venom is poison that is injected through hollow teeth called fangs to kill prey. Venom is made in the body of a snake and is stored in venom sacs. Snakes such as rattlesnakes, with large amounts of venom and large venom sacs, usually have triangular-shaped heads. Snakes such as coral snakes, with small amounts of venom and small venom sacs, do not have triangular-shaped heads.

Snakes do not always need to eat every day or even every week. The larger the animal that a snake eats, the longer the snake can wait until it needs to eat again. Strong acids in a snake's stomach work to digest its food slowly. An anaconda may not eat for months after eating a large pig or deer!

Many people are afraid of venomous snakes. Many people believe that all snakes are venomous, but this is not true. Only about 250 out of 3,000 species of snakes are venomous. That is less than 10 percent of all snakes. Of these 250 venomous snake species, only about 50 of these have venom that is dangerous to people. Still, venomous snakes kill 100,000 people a year. Most of these deaths are from viper (VIE-pur) and cobra bites in the heavily populated parts of Africa and Asia. Australia is the place where the most venomous snakes live. However, fewer than 10 people per year are killed by venomous snakes there. The reason is there are not many people living in Australia.

There are different types of venom. Cobras and coral snakes have venom that poisons the central nervous system. Rattlesnakes and cottonmouths have venom that poisons the blood. Sea snake venom poisons the muscles. All venomous snakebites should be taken seriously. To be safe around all snakes, it is always best to leave them alone.

Snakes
FUNFACT:

In parts of southern Australia, 80 percent of all snakes are venomous. This means that almost any snake you see there will be venomous.

The Saharan sand viper can hide itself in the desert. It buries its body except for its eyes (to see) and its nostrils (to breathe).

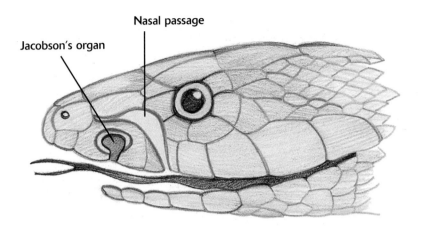

Nasal passage

Jacobson's organ

The Jacobson's organ and nasal passage are highlighted in color above.

Snakes sense the world differently than people do. Snakes do not have ear openings, so they cannot hear. Instead they feel vibrations (vie-BRAY-shuns) from the ground.

Snakes cannot blink because they do not have eyelids. Single see-through scales cover their eyes. When snakes are ready to shed their skins, the scales become foggy. Until the old skin is shed, a snake's vision is not very good. Some snakes that burrow can see very little or are completely blind. Because they spend so much time underground, these snakes do not need to see.

Probably the most important sense for a snake is a combination of taste and smell. A snake's long, forked tongue flicks out to pick up the different scents (SENTS) and flavors in the air. The tongue is then touched to 2 holes in the roof of the snake's mouth. These holes are called the Jacobson's organ (JAY-cub-sunz OR-gen). With the Jacobson's organ, snakes can both taste and smell the air all around them.

Pythons and some other snakes are able to sense heat coming from the body of a warm-blooded animal. Pits along the front edge of these snakes' mouths are very sensitive to heat. By sensing the heat, a snake may feel if a warm-blooded animal, such as a rat or a mouse, is near. This helps them find their food.

The checkered garter snake is a small, non-venomous snake that has good camouflage on the ground.

Most snakes are very good at camouflage (KAM-uh-flaj). Camouflage is the ability to blend into the surroundings to hide. Many snakes have the same colors as the rocks, plants, and dirt where they live. Brown, splotchy-colored snakes are difficult to see in leafy areas. Gray-colored snakes are hard to see in rocky areas. Green snakes are hard to see in bushes and trees.

Some snakes live in many different habitats. They may have different colors, depending on where they live. Other snakes have bright, beautiful colors as a warning that they are venomous. Their yellow, orange, and red colors warn other animals to stay away. Some snakes that are not venomous have bright warning colors. These snakes are called mimics (MIM-iks) because they copy the colors of their dangerous cousins.

Young Amazon tree boas come in 3 different colors: orange, yellow, and rust.

Some snakes change color as they grow. Emerald tree boas, for example, are yellow or red when they are babies and turn green when they are adults.

Horned vipers are the same color as the sand in the deserts where they live, but their camouflage does not end there. They wiggle their bodies into the sand until they are safely buried. The sand keeps them hidden from predators and protects them from the heat of the sun.

Copperheads are colored so that they look like dead leaves lying on the ground, a place where they often hide.

This albino hognose snake plays dead when frightened. It rolls on its back, sticks out its tongue, and even produces a foul odor.

Besides camouflage, snakes have many other ways of defending themselves. Grass snakes roll on their backs and play dead. Hognose snakes play dead and even give off a bad smell. Cobras raise their bodies off the ground and expand the muscles around their necks. This is called hooding and it sends a warning to stay away. Cobras can also spit their venom as far as 3 feet (0.9 meters) in defense. They aim for the eyes of their attacker. This would hurt but not kill the attacker.

Rattlesnakes defend themselves by making a rattling sound as a warning. Cottonmouths show the bright white inside of their mouths. Some snakes may hiss. Others puff out their bodies to look bigger and more frightening. Some snakes even rub their scales together to make a sound like scratchy sandpaper. Ball pythons roll up into a tight ball with their heads hidden in the middle for protection (pro-TEK-shun).

Some snakes live alone most of their lives, so they have to search to find a mate. They use their sense of smell and taste to find each other. Others may hibernate, or sleep through the winter, in large groups and mate when they wake up in the spring. Some of the male snakes wrestle each other for the right to mate with a female snake.

Most snakes have babies by laying eggs. These snakes must find the right place to lay their eggs. Some may lay their eggs in sand. Others lay their eggs in dirt or under rocks. The nest must be in a safe and warm place that is not too wet or too dry.

Baby snakes have a hard knob on their noses called an egg tooth. It is not a tooth at all, but a natural tool that snakes use to tear open their leathery eggs. The egg tooth falls off after the baby has hatched. Usually female snakes lay their eggs and then slither away. The babies must take care of themselves from the time they emerge from the egg.

Pythons are different. Female pythons stay with their eggs. They curl around them to keep them warm and safe. Cobras do not curl around their eggs, but they stay near their eggs to defend them.

Snakes
FUNFACT:

Puff adders may lay as many as 150 eggs at a time. Some blind snakes may lay only 1 or 2 eggs at a time.

This baby black rat snake has just begun to emerge from its shell.

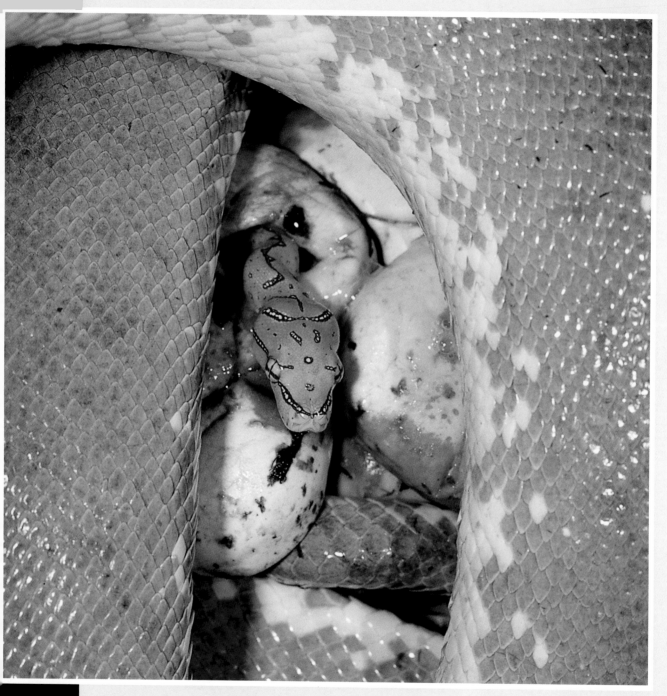

Mother green tree pythons are very unusual because they curl around
their eggs and their hatching babies.

Some snakes give birth to babies that are hatched from soft eggs held inside the mother's body. The babies are wrapped in a thin covering called a membrane. The membrane is not as thick as an eggshell. It is more like a slippery plastic bag. When a baby snake is ready to be born, it slips out of the membrane, out of its mother's body, and is out on its own.

Most water snakes have live born babies because they cannot lay their eggs in water. Most snakes that live in cold climates have live born babies because their eggs would get too cold. Most snakes that live high in trees have live born babies because they cannot lay eggs in a tree.

Snakes live in many different types of places. They live in tropical rain forests, pine forests, and oak forests. They live in swamps, in deserts, in grasslands, and on mountains. They even live where people live, from big cities to farms, ranches, parks, and backyards out in the country. Snakes are shy, though. They stay away from people whenever they can. Snakes are often present but unseen.

Snakes live underground and high in trees, in tall grass and in short grass, in bushes and in barns, underwater and on rocky hillsides. Some of the few places where snakes do not live are New Zealand and Ireland. Both of these countries are islands. This may be a clue as to why there are no snakes in these two places.

Snakes
FUNFACT:

The Martinique thread snake is perhaps the smallest of all snakes. It is about the size and shape of a pencil.

Some scientists say there are 18 groups, or families, of snakes and more than 3,000 species of snakes. Some scientists disagree and say there may only be 14 or 15 families and only about 2,400 species of snakes. No one knows for sure. That is one reason why so many people still study snakes.

No matter how many groups of snakes there are, 4 of these groups are of most interest to people.

Scientists call the largest group of snakes Colubrids (kah-LOO-brids). As many as 70 percent of all snakes may be Colubrids. These snakes are medium-sized. Their right lung is long, but their left lung is either very small or is not there at all. Their heads are covered with large scales. Colubrids may be almost any size, shape, or color. They are found all over the world in many different types of habitats. There are about 1,500 species of Colubrid snakes. Most Colubrids are not venomous, but some are. Most of the venomous Colubrids are not deadly to people.

Milk snakes are harmless snakes that look a lot like coral snakes.
On milk snakes the bands of yellow touch only the bands of black.

One of the venomous snakes in Africa is the boomslang. Its long, slender body can slither gracefully through the tallest trees.

One of the venomous Colubrids is the boomslang, found in Africa. The word boomslang is an Afrikaans (af-ri-KAHNZ) word meaning tree snake. Boomslangs may be gray, black, brown, green, red, or pale blue. These colors make boomslangs hard to recognize. They have thin bodies and may be about 7 feet (2.1 meters) long. They have large eyes and live in trees and bushes where they hunt lizards, a favorite food.

Boomslangs are venomous, but their fangs are in the back of their mouths. That means to kill a lizard they must bite down for a while until the lizard is dead.

San Francisco garter snakes are brightly
colored snakes that are endangered.

King snakes and milk snakes, corn snakes and rat snakes, garter snakes and hognose snakes are all Colubrids that are not venomous. Some of these are among the most colorful and most beautiful snakes in the world.

San Francisco garter snakes have bright red, blue, and black stripes. Most of their habitat is the area where the city of San Francisco now stands. Because of that, there are not many places for these snakes to live, so they are endangered (en-DANE-jurd). They are small, slender snakes that grow to be only about 2 feet (0.6 meters) long. They have large eyes. They feed mostly on fish, toads, and frogs, and they hunt mainly during the daytime.

The green anaconda is the longest snake in the world.

Boids (BOW-idz) are another group of snakes. This group includes boas and pythons, which are alike in many ways. Boids are constrictors. They are not venomous. Instead, they squeeze their prey. Most of them live in tropical parts of the world, places where it is warm all of the time.

Boas live in many parts of the world, including Central and South America. Pythons live only in Africa, Asia, and Australia. Boas hold soft eggs inside their bodies until the babies are ready to be born live into the world. Pythons lay hard-shelled eggs. The longest snakes in the world belong to the Boids group. This includes the reticulated python, Burmese python, carpet python, and the green anaconda, which is a type of boa.

Snakes
FUNFACT:

The yellow anaconda is much smaller than the green anaconda.
It grows to be only about 6 to 10 feet (about 2 to 3 meters) long.

Snakes have many ribs up and down the sides of their flexible spines.

Many Boids have 2 lungs, and many of them have tiny legs that are so small they are almost impossible to see. These legs are not large enough for walking, but they are left over from a long time ago when snakes had legs. Even their skeletons have hips bones, showing that long ago snakes had legs.

The closest relatives to snakes are lizards. Some lizards do not have legs, and some snakes, such as Boids, have tiny legs. How can snakes and lizards be told apart? Lizards have ear openings, and snakes do not.

Boids also have flexible jaws that stretch in the middle of the bottom jaw and expand at the joints. Boids can open their mouths wide and swallow whole the large prey they capture.

Some Colubrids are constrictors, such as the red milk snake.
This snake squeezes a lizard before eating it.

The rainbow boa has dark stripes on its face and head.

The rainbow boa is named for its shiny skin that seems to reflect all of the colors of the rainbow. The colors appear to change as the snake moves and as the light changes. Rainbow boas live in grasslands and in rain forests in South America. They can be found on the ground or in the trees. Young rainbow boas are more colorful than older ones. They all have large eyes and dark lines that run down the center of the head and through the eyes.

These beautiful snakes may have as many as 25 live born babies at a time. Rainbow boas eat birds and small mammals. They grow to be about 6.5 feet (about 2 meters) long.

Another beautiful snake in the Boids group comes from northern Australia and New Guinea (GIH-nee). It is called the green tree python. At just a little over 3 feet (0.9 meters) long, these are not giants at all. They only live high in the trees in the tropical rain forest where they drape, or hang, their bodies over tree branches, and they never come down to the ground. They hunt at night for roosting birds, small mammals, and reptiles. Their color gives them good camouflage.

Green tree python babies are not green. They are bright yellow. This color also gives them good camouflage by making them blend into the sunlight that shines through the leaves in the trees.

Green tree pythons are very similar to emerald tree boas in South America.

Green tree pythons can curl themselves around tree branches as soon as they are born.

This cobra is hooding, or flaring out the
sides of its neck in a display meant to scare.

The third major group of snakes is called the Elapid (eh-LAH-pid) group. Snakes in the cobra family are Elapids. Some of the most dangerous snakes in the world belong to this group, including cobras, coral snakes, sea snakes, and green mambas. Most Elapids have large fangs at the front of their mouths and can inject venom into prey very easily. All of these snakes are venomous. Their venom is very strong. They have slender bodies and large head scales.

The West African green mamba is an Elapid. Although its bite is very dangerous, it is a very shy snake that is rarely seen by people. If it is frightened, it tries to escape. It only bites if it is cornered. The green mamba has large eyes and very large greenish-yellow scales all over its body. It grows to be about 6.5 feet (about 2 meters) long and lives in the forests and woodlands of West Africa. Mambas live up in the trees and use their long, muscular bodies to travel gracefully from one branch or tree to another. This relative of the cobra is an egg-laying snake that eats rats, mice, birds, and even bats.

The Texas coral snake is a much smaller cousin of the mamba and the cobras. Like the mamba, the Texas coral snake is very shy. It has venom that is 8 times stronger than the venom of any other snake in North America. This makes its venom as strong as cobra venom. However, only about 1 percent of all venomous snakebites in America come from these snakes. The reason is that they are very shy and have tiny fangs about one-eighth inch (0.3 centimeters) long.

Coral snakes have beautiful bands of red, yellow, and black. They grow to be about 2 feet (0.6 meters) long. Harmless milk snakes have the same colors, but in a different order. To tell the difference between coral snakes and milk snakes, just remember that coral snakes have bands of red touching bands of yellow. Harmless milk snakes have bands of red touching bands of black.

Coral snakes live in dry pine and oak forests and in thorny scrub, an area where there are low trees and bushes. Coral snakes hide under rocks and fallen leaves.

Venomous coral snakes have bands of red that touch bands of yellow.
That is how people can tell them from the similar-looking but harmless milk snake.

This Gaboon viper is sitting perfectly still on the floor of the forest waiting for its prey.

The last major group of snakes are the vipers. Vipers are snakes with large fangs at the front of the mouth. When they are not in use, their fangs fold back and out of the way. These special fangs can deliver a lot of venom very quickly. This makes vipers dangerous and deadly snakes.

Vipers have many small scales on their heads and heat-sensing pits between each eye and nostril. This helps them to sense warm-blooded animals nearby that might make good prey. The pupils of vipers' eyes are long, thin slits. Venomous snakes such as adders, rattlers, cottonmouths, and copperheads are all vipers.

The Gaboon viper of West and Central African forests and forest clearings is a much-feared viper. It is only about 3 feet 3 inches (1 meter) long, but it has large fangs that can be up to 1.5 inches (3.8 centimeters) long. Its splotchy brown color gives it good camouflage on the forest floor where it can hide in dead leaves and rocks. Its head is large, heavy, and shaped like an arrow. One reason its head is so big is that its venom sacs are so big. The Gaboon viper lies in wait for its prey without moving. When a small mammal comes close, the Gaboon viper strikes quickly.

The Gaboon viper has a very thick, heavy body. Its scales are keeled. That means they are thick and stick out from the body. When Gaboon vipers are frightened they hiss and even puff their bodies out to look larger and more dangerous. They may have as many as 60 live born babies at a time.

The western diamondback rattlesnake is also a viper that is greatly feared by people. It is one of the most dangerous snakes in North America because it can be aggressive if it is frightened. It has a large triangular-shaped head because of its large venom sacs.

The western diamondback rattlesnake has large fangs and blotchy skin that makes up a diamond-like pattern. Even with this distinctive (dis-TINK-tiv) pattern, diamondback rattlesnakes are sometimes hard to identify. They can be many different shades of brown, black, and gray to match the surface colors where they live. They grow a new rattle every time they shed an old skin. This may happen as often as 4 times a year. The rattle is a warning, and one that should be heeded. They are dangerous snakes! The western diamondback rattlesnake eats rats, mice, and even jackrabbits.

Snakes
FUNFACT:

Rattlesnake rattles are old scales that rattle together when shaken. Most rattlesnakes have only a few rattles because the old ones fall off.

This western diamondback rattlesnake is ready to strike.
Its fangs and triangular-shaped head hold large venom sacs.

Most snakes, like these black rat snakes, are harmless to people and do an excellent job of controlling pests such as rats and mice.

Snakes are some of the most amazing and misunderstood animals in the world. While it is true that some snakes are venomous, all snakes have an important job to do in the wild. Because they eat so many rats and mice, they help people by controlling these pests. Still, many people believe that "the only good snake is a dead snake." That is because many people do not know about snakes and are afraid of them. The more people learn about these fascinating animals, the more people will come to like and respect them, not fear them. No matter where snakes live, the most important way to protect them is to protect their homes.

One way to protect them and to protect yourself is to leave snakes alone. Most snakebites happen when people try to touch or bother a snake. So to be safe, respect and admire snakes from a distance.

Internet Sites

You can find out more interesting information about snakes and lots of other wildlife by visiting these Internet sites.

www.kidsplanet.org	Defenders of Wildlife
www.enchantedlearning.com	Enchanted Learning
www.extremescience.com/BiggestSnake.htm	Extreme Science
www.nationalgeographic.com/kids/	National Geographic for Kids
www.pbs.org/wnet/nature/victims/	PBS
www.sdnhm.org/exhibits/reptiles/index.html	San Diego Natural History Museum
http://pelotes.jea.com/vensnake.htm	Venomous Snakes
www.kidsgowild.com	Wildlife Conservation Society
www.worldalmanacforkids.com/explore/animals/snake.html	World Almanac for Kids Online

Index

Titles available in the Our Wild World Series:

NORTHWORD
Minnetonka, Minnesota